THE *Wilton* WAY OF MAKING

gum paste flowers

A COMPLETE BASIC COURSE

AS TAUGHT BY

Josefa Elizondo Barloco

EDITED BY EUGENE T. AND MARILYNN C. SULLIVAN

Wilton Enterprises, Inc. Chicago

FIRST EDITION

Library of Congress Catalog Card Number: 74-34565

International Standard Book Number: 0-912696-05-2

Library of Congress Cataloging in Publication Data

Main entry under title:

The Wilton way of making gum paste flowers.

   1. Cake decorating. I. Sullivan, Eugene T., ed. II. Sullivan, Marilynn C., ed. III. Barloco, Josefa Elizondo. IV. Wilton Enterprises.
TX771.W54   641.8 / 653   74-34565
ISBN 0-912696-05-2

ACKNOWLEDGMENTS: Gum paste flowers and trims by Josefa Elizondo Barloco, assisted by Connie Riherd. Cakes decorated under the supervision of Norman Wilton by the following Wilton staff members: Marie Kason, Amy Rohr and Valerie Wozney. Copy editor: Marsha Adduci. Photography: Edward Hois.

Gum paste, sometimes referred to as "candy clay", has been identified with the culinary arts for centuries. Tragacanth gum—often used in the major paste recipe in this book—is mentioned by the very early Roman writers.

Though the medium of this decorative art is old, it has taken on an entirely new and fresh dimension in the hands of Josefa Elizondo Barloco. At Wilton we believe she has done more than any other decorator to perfect the art of forming beautifully realistic flowers from gum paste.

Over a period of more than twenty-five years, Mrs. Barloco has successfully worked at perfecting the art of making gum paste flowers. She began by painstakingly studying the flowers in her garden. She carefully examined a wide variety of species in the most minute detail and then made patterns of each essential part.

The real artistry, of course, comes in the assembly of the flowers. While the cutters developed by Mrs. Barloco save time, they in no way stifle creativity. No two flowers can ever be fashioned exactly alike, even by the most skilled hands! When carefully executed, however, each flower looks as though it had just been picked.

In this basic course you'll not only learn how to make beautiful gum paste flowers, you'll also learn how to use them to the best advantage in decorating cakes.

One friendly word of caution to those who seek to develop true artistry in creating gum paste flowers: the techniques and instructions provided here have been very carefully thought out, tested and retested. Follow the natural progression from lesson to lesson in the order they are given. Study the pictures and directions carefully. Practice each step to perfection before going on to the next—and you, too, will master the art of making excitingly beautiful gum paste flowers.

—NORMAN WILTON

lesson outline

For as long as I can remember I have had an interest in cooking. In the small Mexican village of Villa del Carmen where I was born, it was always a great pleasure to watch my mother make ojarascas, the tiny tea cookies which were cut in an almost endless variety of interesting shapes. The trim little cutters that were used, brought from Spain nearly two hundred years ago, were passed on to me by my mother and I treasure them highly. Bread was baked in large oval brick ovens and, since there were twelve children in our family—six boys and six girls—this was an almost daily experience.

When I was ten years old our family moved to San Antonio where, one by one we all became United States citizens. Though life took on a new pattern, the early and pleasant memories of learning the simplest of culinary arts from my mother stayed with me. It was always in my mind to share my God-given gifts with others. This, because of having my own family, was put off a number of years. I found that giving my full attention to a husband and five children was a very full and rewarding job.

As the children grew to college age I did, however, pray that I might find some way to add to the family income without leaving our home. Almost miraculously, as I now think back, this was the time a cousin in Mexico visited us and brought doll molds for use in forming gum paste and a recipe for gum paste as well. For me this was the start of a whole new adventure in 1946.

I devised my own formula for making sugar flowers. I labored long at this to get just the right consistency and did most of my work at night, after the household quieted down. My first accomplishment was to take fresh flowers from my garden, separate the petals, and trace them on cardboard. After doing this, I would cut the flower petal pattern with a small knife. Through much trial and error I finally devised cutters that greatly simplify the whole process without in any way minimizing the art form of producing beautiful flowers. The cutters, molds and forming sticks which I designed serve as aids. I had never before seen them used.

As people saw my gum paste flowers, decorating cakes and forming bouquets, many of them came to me to ask if I would teach them this satisfying art. This was the start of a series of classes I have taught for more than

25 years. I can honestly say that every one of my students has succeeded in creating beautiful flowers by following my directions, using the cutters and tools, and of course, by diligent practice.

While I took much enjoyment in teaching my classes, I still realized that I could reach only a relatively small number of people because of limitations of time, and the impossibility of many students to travel to my classes. So, when Mr. Wilton suggested that Wilton Enterprises would like to publish a book on my method, I was delighted. Now I could reach thousands of students who otherwise would not have the opportunity to learn how to make gum paste flowers.

Working on this book has been an arduous but joyful task. I am sure that if you follow the directions carefully, starting at the very beginning, you will soon be turning out flowers just as lovely as those pictured in this book. But just one word of advice—you must practice!

I am extremely happy to pass along to you everything I have learned about this art form. No secrets have been withheld. It has long been my wish to pass along to others the gift that God gave me. I hope you find it provides the pleasure and satisfaction it has given me.

JOSEFA ELIZONDO BARLOCO

know your tools

All of the magic of turning gum paste into a floral garden of beauty begins with the cutters you see here. Each designed after the actual flower petal itself, these cutters produce flower shapes so close to nature they almost appear to be real! The leaf cutter too produces lifelike leaf shapes.

Once you master the art of creating fabulous gum paste flowers you'll be making them for all sorts of special occasions; therefore all of the cutters are carefully crafted from stainless steel to last for years.

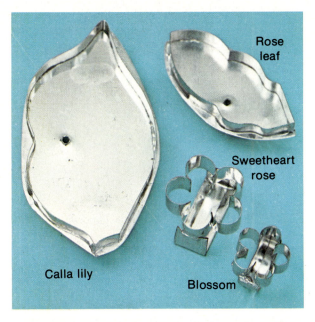

Rose leaf

Sweetheart rose

Calla lily

Blossom

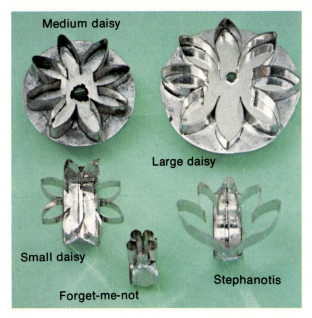

Medium daisy

Large daisy

Small daisy

Forget-me-not

Stephanotis

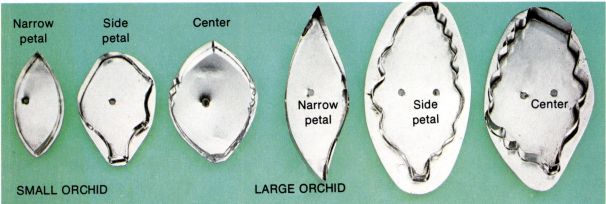

Narrow petal

Side petal

Center

Narrow petal

Side petal

Center

SMALL ORCHID

LARGE ORCHID

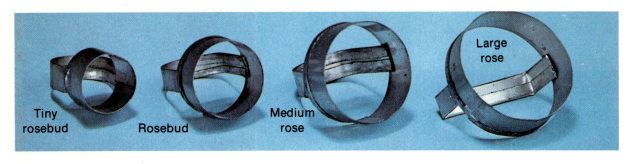

Large rose

Tiny rosebud

Rosebud

Medium rose

A collection of modeling tools

Wooden modeling sticks, numbered consecutively from the largest to the smallest, are the tools that give the gum paste flowers their characteristic shapes.

STICK NUMBER 1—used as a base for curling calla lily, petunia and orchid petals.

STICK NUMBER 2—used to shape and curl rose petals.

STICK NUMBER 3—used to curl petals of spring blossoms and sweetheart roses.

STICK NUMBER 4—used to curl and ruffle carnation, petunia and orchid petals and also used to roll out spring blossom petals.

STICK NUMBER 5—this, the smallest modeling stick, is used to curl the daintiest flower petals including the aster, chrysanthemum and daisy.

A small rolling pin

An important tool, the rolling pin initiates all the pretty floral varieties you'll learn to make, because it's used to roll out the gum paste to just the right thickness for flower cutting.

Two plastic molds

The tools that give gum paste petals and leaves their characteristic markings.

ORCHID MOLD—used to stamp orchid centers and the orchid's two outer ruffled petals.

LEAF MOLD—used to imprint leaves for roses and other floral arrangements.

In addition to the special cutters, modeling tools and molds, there are several other basic supplies essential to creating all the gum paste flowers and arrangements featured in this book. So, before you begin any lesson, be sure you have all these materials on hand.

Some of these supplies you probably have in your own kitchen—others can be purchased at art supply, florist supply, craft and novelty shops.

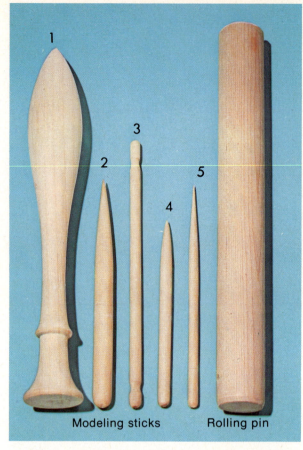

Modeling sticks   Rolling pin

Orchid mold

Leaf mold

Other essentials for creating gum paste flowers:

CORNSTARCH—used to dust work surface before rolling out gum paste.

GUM PASTE INGREDIENTS—Gum-tex™ or tragacanth gum, lemon juice, glucose, powdered sugar.

EGG WHITE—used as gum paste adhesive.

FLORIST WIRE—white and green wire used for flower stems; #24 wire for medium and large flowers, #30 wire for small flowers.

FLORIST TAPE—white and green tape used to wrap stamens and assemble flowers.

NYLON ROPE—used to make flower stamens.

ARTIFICIAL STAMENS—used as petunia centers.

CRYSTAL SUGAR—used to decorate stamens. Can be purchased from a candy supplier or manufacturer.

FINE MESH SCREENING—stamp for daisy centers.

PAPER CONES—used to dry gum paste calla lilies, petunias and orchids.

STYROFOAM—used to dry stamens and flowers.

CURVED FLOWER FORMERS—used to dry and shape orchid petals.

FOOD COLORS—used to tint gum paste.

DRY TEMPERA COLORS—used to tint calla lily and orchid centers.

ARTIFICIAL LEAVES—used to accent flowers.

SATIN RIBBON— to decorate corsages and bouquets. Buy 1½-inch and ¾-inch widths of non-woven ribbon.

TULLE—used to arrange flower corsages and bouquets.

SCISSORS—used to cut ribbon, rope, tulle and tape.

GLASS OR PLASTIC CONTAINERS—used to cover gum paste flower cuts to prevent drying.

PLASTIC BAGS—used to wrap and store gum paste to prevent drying.

ONE-INCH BRUSH—used to dust cornstarch.

ARTIST BRUSH—used to apply dry tempera color.

WIRE CUTTERS—used to cut florist wire and fine mesh screening.

RAZOR BLADE—single edge safety blade used to cut flower petals.

get ready to begin

Gum paste recipe

1 tablespoon Gum-tex™ or tragacanth gum
1 heaping tablespoon glucose
3 tablespoons warm water
1 tablespoon lemon juice
1 pound powdered sugar (or more)

Mix warm water and glucose until glucose is absorbed. Add the gum and lemon juice and, after these ingredients are thoroughly mixed, add small amounts of powdered sugar until you can work the mixture with your hands. Continue adding small amounts of powdered sugar as you knead the mixture on a table top. As soon as the mixture is pliable and can be shaped without sticking to your fingers, you've added enough sugar (a pound or more) and the gum is of correct working consistency.

If you're not going to use the gum paste mixture immediately, place it in a plastic bag and then in a covered container to prevent drying. When stored properly, your gum paste will keep for several months. Gum paste handles best when it is several days old.

How to color gum paste

Once you've made the gum paste recipe, you can tint it any color you desire, or divide the mixture and tint it several different colors.

To color gum paste, apply small amounts of liquid or paste food color with a toothpick. Then with your hands, knead and work the color into the gum paste piece until the tint is evenly applied. If you would like a deeper shade, you can add more color a little at a time, and re-work the gum paste until you achieve the desired shade. Remember, you can always darken a color easier than you can lighten one.

How to roll out gum paste

Always dust your work surface with cornstarch first! This is standard procedure for rolling out gum paste to cut any floral shape. After your work surface is adequately dusted, take a small piece of gum paste, work it

awhile with your hands and then place it on the cornstarch-covered area. Now dust more cornstarch on the surface of your rolling pin and roll out gum paste until it's the thickness you desire—this is usually about 1/16-inch for most flowers. Remember, roll out one small piece of gum paste at a time to avoid drying; and cover every petal and flower cut you make.

How to hand-work gum paste

When you remove gum paste from a plastic bag or covered container, you will need to re-work it with your hands until it's soft and pliable once again. If the gum paste has been stored for some time and seems a little stiff, add a small piece of freshly made gum paste and then re-work it with your hands.

Important reminders:

ALWAYS dust work surface, rolling pin and your hands with cornstarch when handling gum paste and flower cuts.

ALWAYS keep gum paste and flower cuts covered to prevent drying.

ALWAYS add food coloring in small amounts until you achieve the gum paste tint you desire.

ALWAYS re-work gum paste before rolling it out to cut flowers and, if the gum paste has been stored for sometime, add a small piece of freshly made gum paste and re-work until pliable.

lesson one

a spray of spring flowers

Calla lilies, spring blossoms and sweetheart roses gathered into a ribboned corsage dress up a party cake for a special day.

In this, your very first lesson, you will learn how to make each of these three flowers, as well as how to assemble the corsage and decorate a sunny-sweet cake like this! Once you see that you can do it, you'll be eager for all the pretty flower-making lessons to follow.

Making the calla lily

Like any other gum paste flower you learn to make, the calla lily requires practice before perfection is achieved. However, if you carefully follow each step in the flower-making procedure, in a short time you'll be creating calla lilies as breathtaking as Mrs. Barloco's.

MAKE THE STAMEN FIRST. Take a six-inch length of wire and fold one end ¼-inch as shown. Dip this fold in egg white and insert it into an elongated piece of yellow-tinted gum paste. Roll gum paste with your fingers until it extends about two inches on the wire; then brush it with egg white and roll it in yellow crystal sugar. Insert in styrofoam to dry.

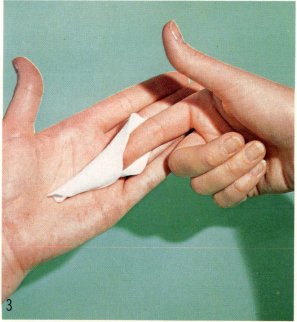

CUT OUT FLOWER. Dust work surface with cornstarch and roll out gum paste to 1/16-inch thickness. Use the calla lily cutter to cut petals and, as you work with one petal, keep others covered to prevent drying. Place a petal cut, point forward, on your left palm and brush egg white from point A to point B.

OVERLAP PETAL. Fold petal side AB to overlap side C as shown, then use your fingers to press the two sides together until the joining seam is smooth. Now you have the basic shape of the flower and you're ready for the next step.

CURL THE PETAL. Once you've mastered the basic shape of the lily, place the flower over the large stick number 1 as shown and, with your fingers, fold the petal edges back. When you've completed this curling, place the flower on a cone to dry. All you have to add is the color and the stamen and you have your first flower.

BRUSH THE THROAT. After the calla lily has thoroughly dried, use an artist brush to paint the inner throat with yellow dry tempera color as shown. It's this sunny color that gives the calla lily its true personality. Now for the final step.

ADD THE STAMEN. Brush egg white around the base of the stamen and insert wire end into the flower. Pull the wire through until the stamen is in place; then wrap a green-tinted piece of gum paste around the base of the flower and insert in styrofoam to dry.

How to make a spring blossom

START WITH STAMENS. Place a strand of nylon rope at one end of a six-inch length of wire so it overlaps the wire ¼-inch as shown. Wrap the rope and wire together with florist tape, making sure to wind the tape down onto the wire so stamens remain in place.

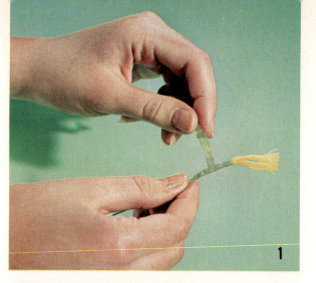

TRIM STAMENS AND CUT FLOWERS. Cut the rope so it extends beyond wire ¾-inch; then separate the strands, dipping the tips first in egg white, then in crystal sugar. Insert in styrofoam to dry. Roll gum paste to 1/16-inch thickness and cut flowers using blossom cutter.

CURL PETALS. Take one flower cut, keeping the others covered to prevent drying, and place it on your left palm. Now, using the rounded end of stick number 3, press each tiny petal from tip to center of flower, causing it to curl.

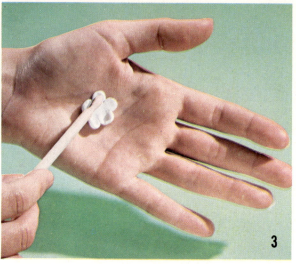

OR ROLL OUT PETALS. A variation for the spring blossom is to round out petals. For this effect, use round end of stick number 4 and roll it from side to side over each petal as shown. When you've shaped all five petals, you're ready to add stamens.

THE FINISHED FLOWER. However you've chosen to shape the blossom's petals, the final step is the same. Brush egg white on the flower's center and insert the wire end of the stamens. Pull the wire through until petals meet stamens; then set aside to dry.

How to make a sweetheart rose

FOLD WIRE, CUT FLOWERS. Take several six-inch lengths of florist wire and fold one end of each wire ¼-inch as shown. Next, roll out gum paste and use sweetheart rose cutter to cut out flowers. As you work with one flower cut at a time, keep other flowers covered to prevent drying.

CURL PETALS. Use round end of stick number 3 to curl petals just as you did for the spring blossom; then make a razor cut between two of the petals that extends to the flower center. Brush egg white on the flower center and slide in wire fold.

FOLD PETALS. Roll the petal to the right of the wire over the petal to the left of the wire, and continue folding petals counterclockwise until you've formed the center bud of the rose. Insert this bud in styrofoam to dry.

CURL MORE PETALS. Use stick number 3 to curl a second set of flower petals just as you did for the rosebud, but do not make any razor cuts in this second set of flower petals.

ASSEMBLE THE ROSE. Now brush egg white in the center of the second curled flower and insert the wire end of the rosebud. Pull wire through until outer petals touch inner bud, add three small pieces of green gum paste below flower and dry rose in styrofoam.

13

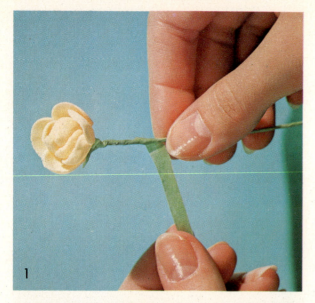

How to make a party cake corsage

In any floral gum paste corsage, the flowers are arranged in order of predominance, featuring the larger flower with the smaller, more delicate blossoms surrounding it. This double corsage shows the calla lily as the foremost flower, with the sweetheart roses and spring blossoms as accompaniment. To make a corsage like this you will need three calla lilies, about a dozen sweetheart roses and two dozen spring blossoms. It would also be advisable to make a few extra flowers of each variety to have on hand.

ASSEMBLE SINGLE CORSAGE FIRST. To begin this floral arrangement, wrap florist tape around the base of a calla lily and around the stems of the sweetheart roses and spring blossoms; then assemble the roses and blossoms into four mini-bouquets. Use three roses and a stem of tiny artificial decorator leaves for the two sweetheart bouquets. To assemble, tape the bases of two roses together, then tape a third rose to these first two, staggering the heights of the flowers as you attach them to one another. Finally, position the stem of leaves behind this bouquet and tape in place at the base.

After you've made the sweetheart rose bouquets, assemble two bouquets of spring blossoms following the same procedure. Use five blossoms—a few of each open and closed petal varieties—and a stem of artificial leaves for both arrangements. Then, when you've finished all four bouquets, tape them one by one below and around the calla lily. When all the flowers are assembled, you can adjust their positions by bending the wire stems. To finish, tie this single corsage with a satiny ribbon bow.

DOUBLE THE CORSAGE. For the second half of the corsage, tape the bases of two calla lilies so one is slightly higher than the other. Then assemble a mini-bouquet of four roses and five blossoms and tape to the base of the lilies. Now tape this entire arrangement to the base of the first corsage and your double corsage is ready for cake trimming.

DECORATE THE CAKE. Bake a two-layer oval cake and ice a sunny yellow. Buttercream, the best-tasting, is the recommended icing for cakes; while Boiled and Royal icings are both ideal for all cake decorating techniques. Recipes for these three icings can be found on page 63.

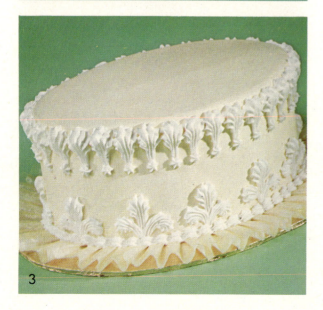

After you've iced the cake, place it on a ruffled-trimmed foiled-covered cardboard that's been cut to a size slightly larger than the cake itself. Then, squeeze out a top border of elongated shells using tube 21, and trim shell bases with tube 16 stars. For the base border, pipe tube 21 fleur-de-lis and shells. Now cut stems of extra flowers and place at the base of the cake with a few artificial decorator leaves. Position the calla lily corsage and your cake will look like springtime itself!

lesson two

a lovely late-summer bouquet

Looking as if they were hand-picked from a garden, gum paste daisies, asters, and chrysanthemums are decoratively arranged in a centerpiece bouquet. In Lesson Two you'll learn the secret of making and arranging these real-looking flowers so you can create a dazzling display like this for friends and family to admire.

And, once you've mastered the art of this beautiful bouquet, you'll be inventing all sorts of attractive floral arrangements of your own!

How to make a large daisy

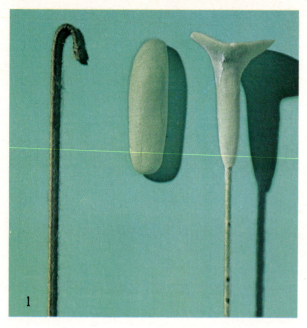

FIRST FORM BASE. Take a six-inch length of wire, fold one end over ¼-inch and insert hook into an elongated piece of green-tinted gum paste; then shape and flatten top of base with your fingers. Note: size of base depends on flower—a large base for a large daisy, a small base for a small daisy.

CUT FLOWER PETALS. Roll out gum paste to 1/16-inch thickness and use large daisy cutter to cut flowers. Next, make two razor cuts in the center of each petal, one deep, one slightly shorter. Note: if you were making the small daisy, you would need only one razor cut per petal.

ROLL FLOWER PETALS. Using the pointed end of stick number 5, roll each petal from side to side enlarging its width. Remember, as you work with one flower cut at a time, keep other daisies and unused gum paste covered to prevent drying.

MAKE STAMENS AND ASSEMBLE FLOWER. Take a small piece of yellow gum paste, shape it into a ball and press it on a piece of fine wire screening. Now brush egg white on flower base, position daisy and attach a stamen, imprinted side up, with more egg white. Dry finished flower in styrofoam.

16

How to make asters

STAMENS COME FIRST. Overlap two strands of nylon rope ¼-inch on the end of a six-inch length of hooked wire, then wrap with florist tape. Be sure to wind tape down onto wire so stamens stay in place. Now cut rope so one inch extends beyond wire and separate strands, dipping tips in egg white, then in crystal sugar.

CUT AND CURL PETALS. Roll out gum paste to 1/16-inch thickness and cut flowers with large daisy cutter. Then make a deep razor cut in the center of each petal and two smaller cuts on either side, so all petals have three cuts. Now press the pointed end of stick number 5 in the center of each petal cut, causing the edges to curl.

DAISIES AND ASTERS

ASSEMBLE THE FLOWER. Brush egg white around the base of the stamens, then insert wire end of stem through the flower's center. Pull wire through until petals meet stamens and you have an aster. Now extend one end of styrofoam beyond edge of work table and insert flower upside down to dry.

How to make a chrysanthemum

START WITH THE STAMENS. Fold one end of a six-inch length of wire ¼-inch; then dip fold in egg white and insert it into a small ball of gum paste. Set stamens in styrofoam to dry; then roll out gum paste and cut flowers with large daisy cutter.

CURL PETALS. Take one flower shape, keeping others covered to prevent drying, and make two razor cuts in the center of each petal—one deep, one slightly shorter. Now place flower on your left palm and curl petals from tip to flower center with the round end of stick number 5.

INSERT STAMENS. Brush egg white on the flower center and insert the wire end of the stamens. Pull wire through until petals come up and around stamens as shown. Now extend one end of your styrofoam base beyond the edge of your work table and insert flower upside down to dry.

CUT AND CURL OUTER PETALS. Two more flower cuts must be curled in order to complete the chrysanthemum. The procedure is the same as for the first inner set of petals, including the upside-down drying between petal additions. As you attach petal rows, use the round end of stick number 5 to curve petal ends up and around flower. Dry finished mum upside down.

How to arrange a summer bouquet

PREPARE FLOWER BOWL. Cut a styrofoam ball to fit bowl for your arrangement; Ice styrofoam in place and cover with green icing. For the next step you will need to make about a dozen gum paste mums and asters along with a dozen and a half assorted size daisies, referring to directions on pages 16-18.

ARRANGE FLOWERS. As you make the flowers for this arrangement, attach them to 12-inch florist wires, taping all stems. Then, begin inserting the more predominant flowers into the center of the styrofoam base to form the structure of your bouquet.

FILL IN ARRANGEMENT. As you work towards the front and sides of this arrangement, clip the wire stems of the flowers making them different lengths. Continue positioning the more predominant flowers first, and then adding smaller blooms to the front and sides of the arrangement, filling in all the open spaces.

ADD LEAVES TO FINISH. When you've attractively arranged all the varieties of flowers, add a few stems of artificial decorator leaves to complete the full effect. Now place your refreshing late-summer bouquet out for all to enjoy! It will last for months and makes a most thoughtful gift too!

lesson three

A breathtaking rose corsage

The daintiest of rosebuds and the fullest of roses are gathered in tulle and tied up with ribbon to make a corsage any florist would be proud to display.

Once you master the making of these floral favorites, as instructed in this lesson, you can arrange a corsage as beautiful as this one. It will surely be treasured by the lucky person who receives it!

A beautiful rose starts with the bud

CUT TWO PETALS. Roll out gum paste to 1/16-inch thickness and, with the small rosebud cutter, cut two round petals. Roll petals into oval shapes, slightly wider at one end, with stick number 2.

PREPARE THE CENTER. Take a six-inch length of wire, fold one end ¼-inch and dip fold in egg white. Insert this fold into a piece of gum paste that has been shaped as a center bud.

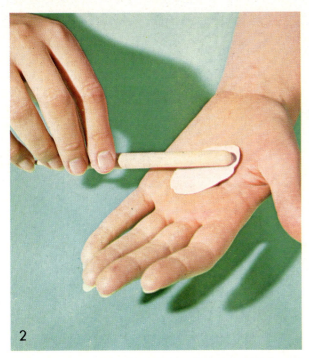

CURL PETALS, ASSEMBLE BUD. Place each petal on your left palm and, once again using round end of stick number 2, curl the wider petal edge as shown. After you've curled both petals, glue one atop the other with egg white. Now turn curled petal edges away from you

and to the left; then center inner bud and wire atop these petals. Fold flat right side of petals down around bud first, then brush on egg white and fold left curled side of petals around to cover right side. Shape three tiny green gum paste pieces around bud base and dry.

How to make a rose

There are three basic steps to making a gum paste rose. First you make a rosebud just as you did on the previous page, second you add an inner row of three petals and third you add an outer row of six petals. Making a beautiful rose requires practice, but if you carefully follow each step you'll achieve success.

CUT THREE INNER PETALS. After you've made a rosebud, as shown on page 21, cut three petals using the small rosebud cutter. Use the round end of stick number 2 to roll the petals into oval shapes, slightly wider at one end, just as you did for the bud.

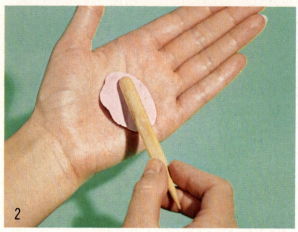

CURL PETALS. Place petals, one at a time, on your left palm and once again use the round end of stick number 2 to curl wider petal edges as shown. When you've curled all three petals you're ready for the next step.

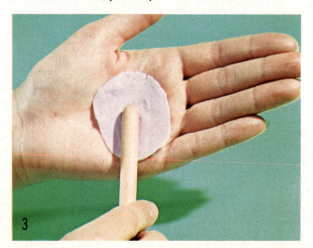

ADD PLEATS. Place petals, one at a time, on your left palm with curled edges away from you. Then, roll the round end of stick number 2 in the petal's center, brush egg white on the petal base and make a center pleat with your fingers.

POSITION PETALS. After you pleat each petal, hold rosebud upside down and attach pleated end to the bud's base so petal edges curl outward. Add remaining two inner petals the same way, positioning them from pleat to pleat.

5

PREPARE OUTER PETALS. Since you've already made the rosebud and inner rose petals, this last step will be easier. Cut and roll six petals into oval shapes, just as you did for the bud and first set of petals. Then, with the round end of stick number 2, curl the wider ends of each petal as before.

6

7

PLEAT AND POSITION PETALS. After you've curled all six petals, roll the centers with stick number 2 and pleat the petal bases. Insert rose upside down in styrofoam and attach outer petals positioning them from pleat to pleat around the base of the inner petals.

DRY FINISHED FLOWER. When all the petals are in place and the rose is complete, place the finished flower in a container filled with powdered sugar or cornstarch, open and shape the petals and let dry overnight.

After you've mastered the rosebud and rose-making procedures, you're ready to start a stunning corsage. You will need to make about a half-dozen roses and buds, wrapping the wire stems with florist tape. As you finish each flower, stand it in styrofoam so you can keep count of how many you've made.

How to create a rose corsage

FIRST MAKE TULLE BUTTERFLIES. Cut 3-inch wide net tulle into half-yard lengths; then take one piece and gather net together at the center with your fingers. Next, place a six-inch length of wire behind the net and fold one end tightly over the gathered center without twisting the wire.

NEXT MAKE BOWS. For large flowers, make three 2¾-inch wide ribbon loops starting with a long end and ending with a short end. To finish tie in one more long end piece. Use 1½-inch wide ribbon for medium size bows and for small bows, split ¾-inch wide ribbon to any width; then loop, twist wire around base and tape.

START CORSAGE. Make about a half-dozen roses and buds with inner petals only referring to directions on pages 21-23; then tape all flower stems. Make a loop of tulle for a flower backing and twist on wire at base wrapping with tape. Start taping flowers together to this net positioning each one a little lower as shown.

ADD ON FLOWERS, TULLE AND RIBBONS. As you add to the corsage, alternate taping on buds, roses, tulle and ribbon until your corsage is full; then tie it up with a big ribbon bow as shown. With your corsage complete, you can present it to someone dear to highlight a special date or occasion.

lesson four

A tall silver goblet filled with ruffled petunias and grass-green leaves makes a bright arrangement for a special table setting. Once you learn how to make the pretty petunias, the rest is very easy.

a mini-bouquet of petunias

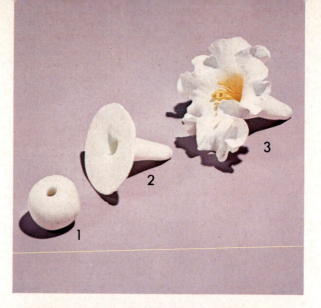

How to make a ruffled petunia

This frilly flower is shaped in three basic steps without the use of a special cutter. First, you form a ball base, second you shape the ball into a wide hollowed well and third you curl petals adding color and stamens.

Since there is no special cutter for this flower, you will need to practice each of the steps several times until you achieve satisfactory results.

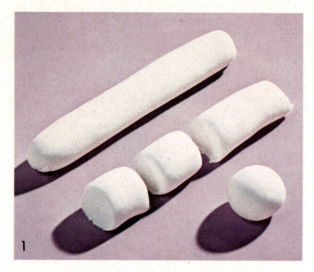

FORM BALL BASE. Roll a small piece of gum paste into a long tube shape and divide in three equal pieces. Take one of the three pieces and form a ball shape with your fingers as shown. Now for the next step.

MAKE A CENTER HOLE. Use the round end of stick number 4 to hollow out a hole in the center of the ball base as shown above. Hold the ball in one hand and, with the other hand, roll the stick around to form hole.

ENLARGE CENTER HOLE. After you've hollowed a center hole, continue rolling the stick and gradually work outward, enlarging the outer edges of the ball base as shown.

FORM A WELL. After you enlarge this flower base, press and shape the outer edges with your fingers until you have a cone-shaped well as shown. Now you have the basic shape of the flower.

RUFFLE PETAL EDGES. Place the flower you've just shaped in your left hand, and make a half-closed fist so the cup-shaped outer edges of the flower rest atop your fingers. Now use the pointed end of stick number 4 to ruffle the flower's edges as shown. This procedure may seem awkward to you at first, but as you practice, this petal ruffling will become second nature.

CURL RUFFLED PETAL. After you've ruffled the edges of the flower, invert the petunia on stick number 1 and, with your fingers, alternately bend the ruffles up and down to give the flower a more natural look.

DRY FLOWER. Set the petunia on a cone to dry as shown; then follow the same shaping, ruffling and curling procedures to make flowers from the remaining two tube-shaped gum paste pieces.

ADD STEM AND COLOR. When the petunia is dry, insert a six-inch length of hooked wire into the base and secure with florist tape. Now use an art brush to paint on dry tempera color giving the petunia its personality.

ADD STAMENS. For the final step, take three to six artificial stamens and fold in half. Dip the folds in egg white and position them in the petunia's brightly colored center; then set flower aside to dry.

How to make leaves

CUT AND MOLD. Roll out green-tinted gum paste to about 1/16-inch thickness and cut out leaf with the leaf cutter. Place leaf cut over leaf mold and press into indentations to stamp on vein markings. Remove leaf from mold and you're ready to attach the wire stem.

ADD STEM. Turn leaf cut so that vein marks are face down; then brush egg white down the center of the leaf. Position a six-inch length of wire over this brushed area and fold base of leaf cut over wire. Now turn leaf right side up and bend wire to shape. Dry on curved form.

PREPARE GOBLET. Cut a ball of styrofoam to fit goblet or container in which you wish to arrange flowers then ice it a light green. Secure it in the container with icing. Make about a dozen gum paste petunias, referring to directions on page 26 and 27, along with several leaves.

ARRANGE FLOWERS. After you've taped the wire stems of all flowers and leaves, begin inserting petunias into the styrofoam base, clipping the wires to different lengths. Position shorter flowers in the front of the arrangement, taller flowers towards the back. With flowers in place add a few leaves to complete.

Fresh as a garden, this silver vase is filled with gum paste asters, daisies, roses, carnations and blossoms. Certainly a dramatic arrangement for a table centerpiece and one bouquet you'll learn how to make and assemble in this lesson.

lesson five

How to make a carnation

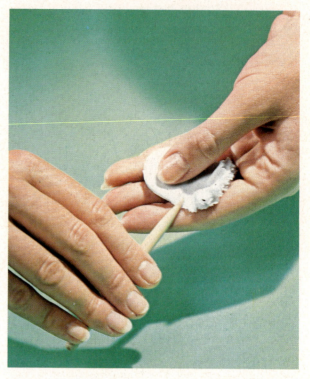

CUT PETALS. Roll out your gum paste to ¼-inch thickness and use the largest rose cutter to cut out flowers. As you work with one flower at a time, keep other gum paste cuts covered to prevent drying.

RUFFLE PETALS. Place one of the flower cuts on your left palm and use the pointed end of stick number 4 to ruffle the outer edges of the flower cut as shown. Since you've already mastered the petunia, this ruffling should seem easier to you.

COMPLETE THE FLOWER. Brush egg white on the center top half of the flower and fold the lower half over it as shown in step 1. Next, brush egg white on the fold and position a six-inch wire that has been folded ¼-inch and dipped in egg white. See step 2. Now fold the right half of the flower over the wire, brush on more egg white, and fold the left half of the flower over the right half. See steps 3 and 4. To finish, smooth the flower base onto the wire and set aside to dry.

Get flowers ready for arrangement

To create the dramatic arrangement on page 29, you will need to make about two dozen spring blossoms, one dozen large daisies and carnations and about a half-dozen roses and asters. Use 12-inch wires for stems. In addition to the flowers, make about a dozen gum paste leaves. Note: it's always advisable to make extra flowers and leaves in case of breakage. Tape all stems with florist tape and insert in styrofoam.

How to arrange the bouquet

PREPARE VASE. Cut a piece of styrofoam to fit flower vase and ice green. Position the more predominant flowers first cutting the wire stems to different lengths as shown. As you position some of the larger flowers, such as the rose, tape a few leaves to its base, then insert it into the styrofoam as shown. Continue placing shorter flowers to the front of the arrangement, taller flowers to the back.

FILL IN WITH MORE FLOWERS AND LEAVES. Continue positioning flowers of different stem lengths to fill out arrangement, adding leaves between. As you add flowers, take care so as to avoid breaking the delicate gum paste petals. When your bouquet is nice and full like the one shown, place it on a table or another appropriate focal point to serve as a decorative centerpiece. This arrangement, like others you have made, will last for months of enjoyment by your family and friends!

lesson six

a radiant bridal bouquet

The orchid, admired by all, is the stunning feature in this glamorous bridal bouquet. Accented by stephanotis and delicate forget-me-nots, this fanciful floral arrangement is one any bride-to-be would treasure!

33

How to make stephanotis

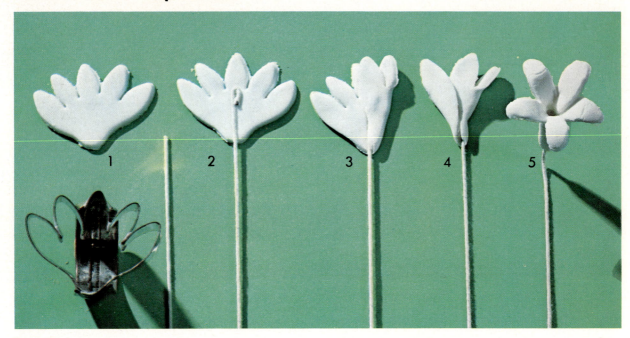

CUT FLOWER, ATTACH WIRE AND FOLD. Roll out gum paste and use the stephanotis cutter to cut flower petals. Take one flower cut, keeping others covered to prevent drying, and brush egg white on the left side of the flower from tip to base. Next, take a six-inch length of wire, fold one end ¼-inch and dip fold in egg white. Position wire directly under flower's center petal as shown in step 2. Now fold the right side of the flower over the wire; then fold the left side of the flower so it meets the center petal as shown in steps 3 and 4. Smooth flower base onto wire with your fingers, and fold petal tips outward to finish stephanotis.

How to make forget-me-nots

CUT FLOWER, CURL PETALS AND ADD STAMENS. Roll out gum paste and use the forget-me-not cutter to cut the tiny flowers. Work with one flower cut at a time, keeping others covered to prevent drying. Place flower cut on your left palm and use the round end of stick number 5 to curl petals. See step 2. Now, brush egg white on back of flower and attach wire by inserting one end just barely through flower center as shown. Dot center with yellow royal icing for the stamen and insert flower in styrofoam to dry.

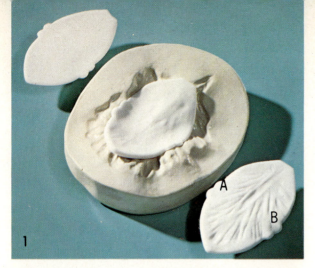

How to make a medium-sized orchid

The orchid is probably the most difficult flower you will learn to make; however with patience and practice you will be able to create orchids as stunning as the ones in the bridal bouquet.

There are four basic steps to making an orchid of any size: (1) inner throat, (2) ruffled leaves, (3) narrow leaves and (4) flower assembly. Practice each step carefully and you'll master them all.

Medium orchid: STEP ONE: MAKE THE THROAT

1. CUT AND STAMP PETAL. Roll out gum paste to 1/16-inch thickness and use the center cutter for the small orchid to cut inner petal for orchid throat. Place this petal over the orchid mold as shown and press it into the mold indentations to imprint veins.

2. RUFFLE PETAL. Dust cornstarch over the petal and over your left hand; then place petal, point forward and vein side up, on your palm. Use the pointed end of stick number 4 to ruffle petal edges from point A to point B as shown.

3. POSITION WIRE. Turn the ruffled petal over so vein markings are face down and brush egg white along the left side of the petal from beginning of ruffle to base. Place a six-inch length of wire over this brushed area as shown, and you're ready to shape the throat.

4. FORM THROAT. Hold petal and wire between right thumb and forefinger so vein-stamped side is away from you. Now with your left hand, fold the other side of the petal over to the wire side so veins appear in the center. Now you have the basic shape of the orchid's throat.

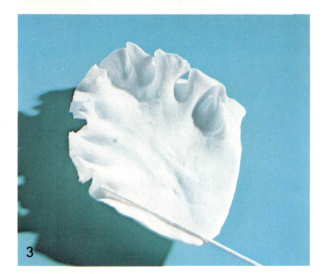

Medium orchid: STEP ONE CONTINUED

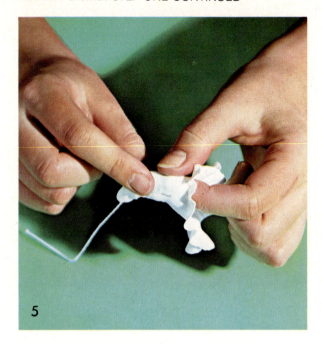

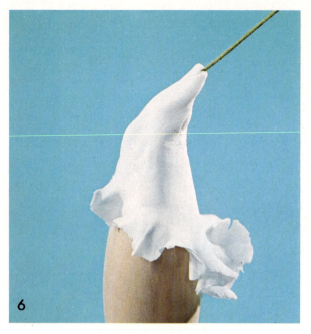

5. SECURE SIDES. After you've joined both sides of the throat, insert the pointed end of stick number 4 into the throat and continue to press sides together all the way down to the throat base. Now with your fingers, build a small ridge of gum paste over the wire.

6. SHAPE RUFFLES. Place the orchid throat over stick number 1 as shown and alternately bend ruffled petal edges up and down to give the orchid center a more natural look. Now place the throat over the point of a cone to dry overnight.

Medium orchid: STEP TWO: MAKE RUFFLED SIDE PETALS

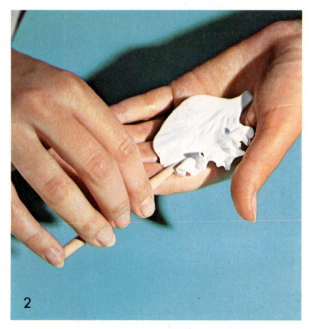

1. CUT AND STAMP PETALS. Roll out gum paste and use the small orchid side petal cutter to cut out two petals. One at a time place petals over the orchid mold as shown and press into mold indentations to imprint veins.

2. RUFFLE PETALS. Dust the petals and your left hand with cornstarch; then place a petal, point forward vein side up, on your left palm. Use the pointed end of stick number 4 to ruffle petal edges from point A to point B as shown. Do the same for the other petal cut.

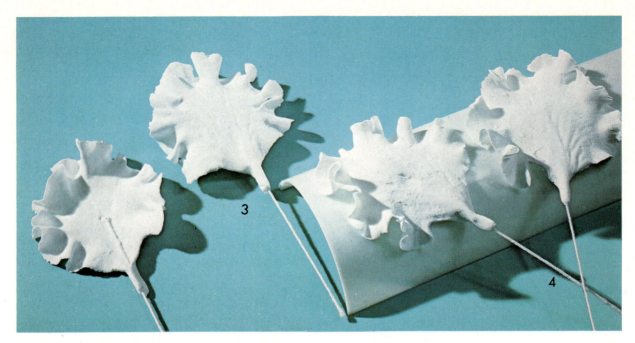

3. ATTACH WIRE. Turn petal cuts over so vein prints are face down and brush egg white down the petal centers. Position six-inch florist wires over the brushed areas and fold the petal bases over the wires as shown.

4. DRY DIAGONALLY. Place curled petals over curved flower formers and dry diagonally as shown overnight. Now you're ready for the third step.

Medium orchid: STEP THREE: MAKE NARROW PETALS

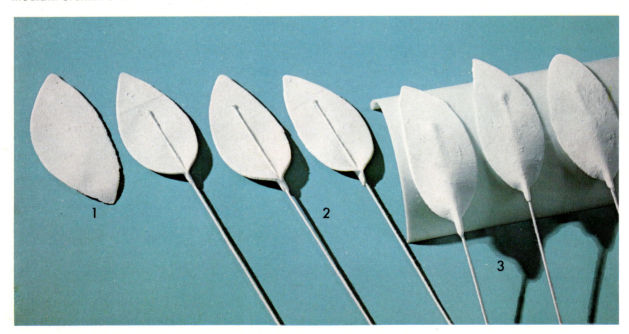

1. CUT PETAL. Roll out gum paste and use the narrow petal cutter for the small orchid to cut three petals.

2. ATTACH WIRE. Turn petals over and brush egg white down the centers; then position six-inch wires over the brushed areas and fold petal bases over wires as shown.

3. SHAPE AND DRY. Bend petals and wires to shape as shown, then dry the narrow petals straight up and down on a curved flower former overnight.

1. TAPE PETALS AND THROAT. Before you tape the separate flower parts together, wrap the stems of the narrow and ruffled petals with florist tape as shown. Next, tape the base of the orchid throat, winding tape about halfway down wire.

2. ADD COLOR. Dust cornstarch off of the orchid throat, then brush on dry color starting from the inside and working out. You can brush on any color you like, but yellow and purple are the most popular.

3. TAPE THROAT AND RUFFLED LEAVES. Position a ruffled petal on both sides of the orchid throat and wrap stem bases together with florist tape, starting below the petals' own tape lines.

4. ADD NARROW PETALS. Tape the narrow petals to the throat and side petals, positioning one petal behind the orchid and two petals in front of the orchid as shown. Now you're ready to add the stamen.

5. MAKE THE STAMEN. Take a piece of gum paste and round it to about an inch length; then place it over the round end of stick number 4. Shape the gum paste halfway around the stick and remove it. Now make one tiny razor cut on each side of the stamen and reposition it on stick number 4. Fold the top half of the stamen over the round end of the stick and make three dots with a felt-tipped marker. To attach, brush egg white on the end of the stamen and use the stick to position it in the orchid's throat. Note: insert the stamen into the orchid throat immediately, while stamen is still wet.

Finished orchid! Add ribbon and tulle and you have a corsage!

How to make a large orchid

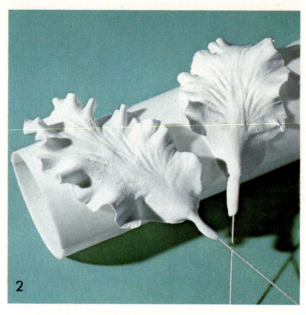

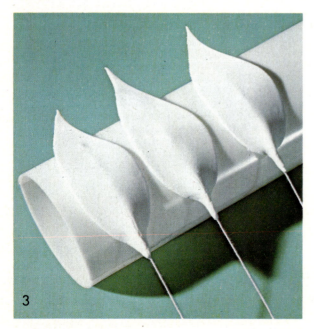

1. MAKE THROAT FIRST. The procedures are the same as for the medium orchid. For the throat, cut center petal with large orchid cutter and place on mold with low and less scalloped side to the left. Press to stamp veins, then curl petal with stick number 4 from second scallop on the left to the center of the second scallop on the right. Attach wire, form throat and dry overnight on stick number 1.

2. MAKE RUFFLED PETALS. Now roll out gum paste and cut two large orchid side petals. Ruffle petal edges with stick number 4 just as you did for the medium orchid; then position florist wires and fold the base of the petal cuts over the wire. Dry petals diagonally on a curved former overnight.

3. MAKE NARROW PETALS. Roll out gum paste and cut three large orchid narrow petals. Attach wires with egg white and fold petal bases just as you did for the medium orchid. Place petals straight up and down on a curved former as shown and dry overnight.

4. ASSEMBLE. Once again, just as you did for the medium orchid, make center stamen and assemble flower with florist tape, wrapping the throat and ruffled leaves first. Now tape narrow leaves positioning one behind orchid throat, and two in front. Add stamen to complete.

How to assemble a bridal bouquet

MAKE BOWS, BUTTERFLIES AND FLOWERS. For the beautiful bride's bouquet, you will need to make several tulle butterflies and double loop bows using 1½-inch wide ribbon. In addition to these trims, you will also need to make one large and two medium gum paste orchids, along with three dozen stephanotis and forget-me-nots. Refer to flower-making directions on pages 34-40 and assemble all flowers with white florist wires, wrapping stems with white tape.

MAKE MINI-BOUQUETS AND ASSEMBLE. To start the bridal arrangement, you will need to make six mini-bouquets, each with five stephanotis and five forget-me-nots. Tape stems together as shown positioning forget-me-nots at the front and bending wires slightly. Now wrap ribbon, tulle butterflies and large orchid together with two of the mini-bouquets as shown. Set this top of the bouquet aside as you assemble the rest.

ASSEMBLE MINI-BOUQUETS AND MEDIUM ORCHIDS. Arrange remaining mini-bouquets, ribbon and tulle butterflies around each of the two medium-sized orchids; taping three bouquets to the stem of one orchid, and one bouquet to the stem of the other orchid. One at a time tape each of these orchid arrangements below and on either side of the large orchid as shown. Now you have a stunning bouquet any bride-to-be would cherish.

lesson seven

make cakes more glamorous with gum paste flowers

Peach and plum-pink asters are strewn at the feet of a gay dancing figurine to make a party cake any young girl would fancy! For a birthday or any day, gum paste flowers like these make a cake something very special for everyone.

In this lesson there's a variety of floral cake decorating ideas that put your newly acquired talents to work. Once you've made the flowers for any cake, you'll find you won't have to add too many other trims; and, as you become more expert in making flowers, you'll find you'll be thinking of a variety of delightful cake decorating and party ideas of your own.

How to decorate aster cake

MAKE ASTERS FIRST. Refer to flower-making directions on page 17 and make about a dozen gum paste asters. Note: when making gum paste flowers for any decorating purpose, always make a few extra in case of breakage.

DECORATE THE CAKE. Bake a two-layer, 8-inch square cake and ice a soft yellow. Place the cake on a pretty stand and, with a toothpick, trace a scalloped outline on one cake top corner, draping the outline over and onto the side corners of the cake.

Overpipe the outlines twice with tube 16—once straight, and once using a swirled hand motion giving the scallops a feathered effect. Fill in this outlined area with dots of pink-peach icing using tube 2.

Next, use a toothpick to trace a scalloped outline around the base of the cake, and once again overpipe the outline with tube 16—first straight and then again with a swirled hand motion. Finally add a row of rosettes around the cake base with tube 16.

Now for the flower arranging. Ice a small circle of styrofoam and position it on the cake using a dot of icing to secure in place. Position figurine on styrofoam and pipe a row of tube 16 shells around its base. To attach flowers, trim wire stems first and then position them around styrofoam and cake base with dots of icing. What a special treat for a special someone!

A rose-trimmed cake in the prettiest of party pinks

MAKE GUM PASTE TRIMS FIRST. Before you can decorate a radiant rose cake like this, you have to make the gum paste sweetheart roses. Refer to flower and leaf-making directions on pages 13 and 28; and make about a dozen pink sweetheart roses and leaves. Place your gum paste decorations in styrofoam to dry and then you're ready to start the cake.

DECORATE THE CAKE. Bake a two-layer, 10-inch round cake and ice a frosty pink. Place the cake on a foil-covered cardboard cut to a circle about two inches larger than the cake, and start the trimming.

First pipe a tube 16 shell border around the cake base; then, with a toothpick, trace a scalloped outline around the cake top and base. Overpipe outline once on cake top and twice around cake base using an "i" hand motion with tube 17. At the peak of each scalloped curve, pipe a pretty fleur-de-lis with tube 17; then edge the cake top with a row of tube 16 shells.

To position the dancing ballerina, cut a small circle of styrofoam and ice it pink. Center the styrofoam and dancing figurine on the cake, then cover the styrofoam edges with tube 17.

Now add the flowers. Clip wire stems off leaves and place around ballerina and cake base, attaching with royal icing. Finally, trim rose stems and position with icing, and your cake is party perfect!

A sweetheart of a cake
decked with carnations

A thoughtful treat for Mother's Day or a favorite valentine, this two-tiered heart is trimmed with frills of icing and lacy carnations. Truly a sweet surprise for anyone dear to your heart!

MAKE FLOWERS FIRST. Refer to directions on page 30 and make about two dozen gum paste carnations. While these flowers are drying, make about a dozen gum paste leaves as shown on page 28.

When carnations and leaves are dry, wrap stems with florist tape and assemble into one large bouquet with tulle and three separate mini-bouquets.

DECORATE THE CAKE. Bake two-layer heart cakes, one 12-inch and one 6-inch and ice both a blushing pink. Place cake on a foil-covered cardboard circle and then add icing trims.

Frame cake bases with tube 320 reverse shells and cake tops with tube 347 ripple borders. For cake sides pipe rippled scallops and beading with tube 4; then add stringwork and bows using the same tube.

Position gum paste floral bouquets around the cake tops and sides as shown, then present your sweet show of affection for all to see!

A fresh-as-a-daisy wedding

Fresh-looking as a wedding bouquet, gum paste daisies and sunny carnations adorn a cake made for the bride and groom. Flowers like these are sure to be the stars of the celebration as well as treasured keepsakes for the happy couple.

MAKE FLORAL BOUQUETS FIRST. Refer to flower-making directions on pages 16 and 30 and make about a half-dozen gum paste carnations and two dozen assorted medium and large daisies.

While flowers are drying, refer to leaf-making directions on page 28, and make about a half-dozen gum paste leaves to accent bouquets.

When flowers and leaves are dry, wrap wire stems with florist tape and assemble into one large and three mini-bouquets. Accent large bouquet with tulle and wide 2¾-inch ribbon, small bouquets with 1½-inch wide ribbon. Add a few thin white ribbons to each arrangement; then tape the large bouquet base to a heart-trimmed ornament base.

DECORATE THE CAKE. Bake two-layer, 8-inch, and two-layer, 12-inch round cakes and ice pastel yellow. Assemble cake tiers with 10-inch round separator plates and 10½-inch column pillars, positioning large floral bouquet ornament as shown.

Trim tier bases with tube 199 shell puffs and tube 101 ruffled edging. To complete base borders, frame shell tops with rippled scallops using tube 2 for the small tier and tube 3 for the large tier.

For tier side trims, trace curved lines with a toothpick and overpipe outlines with tube 14, using an up-and-down hand motion to effect zigzag. Complete side borders by adding tiny flowers with tube 1.

To finish decorations, edge separator plate with tube 16 and trim tier tops with tube 199 shells. Top the bridal tribute with an appropriate ornament and place your mini-bouquets around the cake!

A wedding cake abloom with snow-white roses and ice-blue forget-me-nots

Here's a wedding cake decorated in the sweetest of traditions with gum paste flower bouquets that make sentimental mementos of this happiest of days. The decorative filigree trim adds to the radiance, making this a cake to be remembered.

PREPARE THE BOUQUETS. Make about a half-dozen gum paste roses, following directions on pages 21-23, and also make a dozen gum paste forget-me-nots referring to directions on page 34. After you've made the flowers, make a few large leaves following directions on page 28; then make a couple smaller leaves using a pattern. When flowers and leaves are dry, wrap stems with florist tape and assemble into two bouquets.

For one bouquet, tape one rose together with a few forget-me-nots; then tape on a large leaf and a small leaf and add a few ribbon bows. For the cake-top bouquet, tape together three roses, several forget-me-nots, three large leaves and ribbons. Note: trim stems of flowers as you tape them together.

DECORATE THE CAKE. Bake two-layer 8-inch, and two-layer 12-inch square cakes. Ice white and assemble with 10-inch square separator plates and 5-inch plastic filigree-trimmed pillars.

To accent the filigree pillars, cover four plastic filigree shields with clear plastic wrap and pipe over the patterns with tubes 3 and 14 and Royal icing. Let dry overnight, then carefully peel off wax paper and set aside to use as decorations.

Now edge cake tier bases with tube 87, using an up-and-down hand motion. Next, with tube 16, pipe scroll designs on all four side corners of the large base tier. As you pipe scrolls, use a straight hand motion first, then overpipe with a circular motion to achieve a feathered effect. Edge the separator plate with tube 87 and once again use tube 16 to pipe small horseshoe scrolls on the top of the 12-inch tier.

To decorate the 8-inch tier, pipe scrolls on all four cake side corners using tube 16. Pipe the scroll first with a straight hand motion, then overpipe with a circular hand motion. To complete the cake, attach shield designs around the 12-inch tier with icing, and position gum paste bouquets.

lesson eight

dainty mint sugar decorations

Gelatin mint sugar, another versatile type of decorating paste, makes an endless variety of colorful cake trims and party favors; besides being good tasting.

Mint sugar recipe
  3 envelopes unflavored gelatin (3 tablespoons)
  1 cup warm water
  ½ cup cornstarch
  3 pounds powdered sugar
  2 to 3 drops oil of peppermint

Dissolve gelatin in warm water and pour through a fine sieve into a glass bowl. Add 2 to 3 drops of peppermint oil; then blend in cornstarch and a small amount of powdered sugar. Keep adding sugar a little at a time, until the mixture becomes very smooth. When mint sugar is of the correct consistency, store in a tight-covered jar that has been dusted inside with cornstarch.

The very same procedures for tinting and rolling out gum paste are applied to mint sugar. To tint, add small amounts of food color with a toothpick and work into the mixture with your hands.

  To roll out mint sugar, always dust your hands, work surface and rolling pin with cornstarch first; then roll to desired thickness. Cut out decorative pattern pieces immediately, since mint sugar is very quick drying.

How to make baby booties

Unlike the gum paste flowers, mint sugar trims are cut from patterns, and then separate parts are assembled with Royal icing. (Icing recipe on page 63.)

CUT OUT SIDE PIECE. To make the sweet baby booties, roll out mint sugar to about ⅛-inch thickness. Place the side pattern piece over the mint sugar and cut around it with a razor; then drape over curved former as shown. Dry thoroughly.

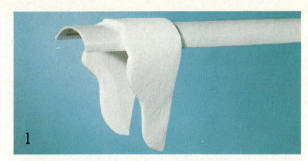

CUT SOLE, ATTACH SIDE. As soon as you've folded the side piece, roll out more gum paste and use other pattern piece to cut out bootie sole and tongue. Brush water around the outer edge of the sole, then position side and fold tongue up and around to meet sides.

POSITION TONGUE, ADD RIBBON HOLES. When the bootie's tongue is folded in place, use your small wooden modeling stick to make four holes—two on either side of the bootie and two on either side of the tongue as shown. Now set bootie aside to dry.

How to decorate the cake

First, you will need to make about two dozen pink and blue spring blossoms as shown on page 12 and a pair of mint sugar baby booties. After you've made these trims, you're ready to decorate.

Bake and ice a two-layer, 8-inch square cake and place on a foil-covered, ruffled-trimmed cardboard that has been cut to a slightly larger size than the cake itself. Now, with a toothpick, trace four curved scrolls on all four cake sides and over-pipe the scrolls with tube 17, using a straight hand motion first, and then going over curves with a swirled hand motion to give scrolls a feathered effect. Next, pipe a few tube 17 rosettes on each corner of the cake and top with tube 17 fleur-de-lis—piping one on each side and top corner. To complete the decorations, pipe a row of rosettes around the base of the cake with tube 504 and write welcome wishes with tube 2. Now place a small piece of styrofoam in each bootie and push in flowers; then place booties atop cake. Cut wire stems off remaining blossoms and place around cake with icing. Finished, you have a special surprise for a new mother!

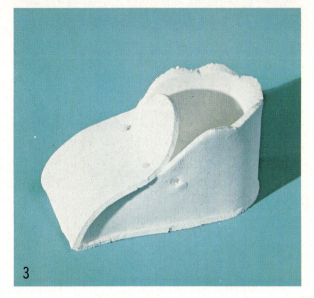

DECORATE WITH ICING AND RIBBONS. To decorate the bootie, use Royal icing and tubes 1 or 2 to squeeze out dainty flowers and dots; then pipe shells with tube 13. When icing trims are dry, insert tiny satin ribbons through holes and tie up in pretty bows. Now you can fill the bootie with colorful gum paste flowers for cake trimming, or add mints and nuts for take-home favors.

a graduate's cap

MAKE CAP AND MORTARBOARD. To form cap, shape a piece of mint sugar around a cup or glass that's about 2 inches in diameter and 2 inches high. Set aside to dry. Now roll out some mint sugar to ⅛-inch thickness and use pattern to cut out mortarboard. Make a small hole in the center and set mortarboard aside to dry also.

ADD TASSEL. When both cap pieces have dried, pull the end of a string tassel up through the center hole in the mortarboard and glue in place underneath with Royal icing. Now you're ready to put the two cap pieces together.

COMPLETE CAP. When tassel is securely positioned, carefully remove cap from its cup or glass form and glue mortarboard in place with Royal icing as shown. When dry, trim all edges with tube 2 beading.

CUT AND ROLL DIPLOMA. Roll out mint sugar to ⅛-inch thickness and use rectangular pattern to cut out diploma. While moist, roll up mint sugar piece to diploma shape and dry. Tie with ribbon.

How to decorate the cake

First, you will need to make about a dozen gum paste asters as shown on page 17, along with a mint sugar graduate's cap and diploma. When these trims are ready, it's on to the cake.

Bake and ice a two-layer, 9-inch star cake, then place it on a foil-covered cardboard that's been cut to a star shape slightly larger than the cake itself. Next, use tube 16 to pipe a row of rosettes around the cake top and base and down each star point; then add trios of tiny rosette triangle designs to the side of each star point—at both the top and base.

To finish the trimming, position cap and diploma; then trim wire stems of gum paste flowers and attach with icing. When completed, this is one graduate cake that's destined to be the star of a party!

a rock-a-bye cradle

How to decorate the cake

First you will need to make a mint sugar cradle as shown on the opposite page, and about one dozen gum paste roses and a half-dozen buds.

These flowers are made in a different way than regular roses. Form the center of the flower as directed in step three, page 13. Then add petals, cut with the rosebud cutter, just as you would for a regular rose. The buds are made just as step three, page 13 indicates, with green calyx added. You'll like this dainty version of the rose.

Bake a two-layer, 9-inch petal cake and ice the top white and the sides mint green. Position the cake on a round party plate and decorate! Pipe puffy garlands around each petal curve at cake top and base with tube 16, making each of the garlands proportionate to the curve of the cake. Next, overpipe garlands at cake top with a triple row of tube 2 stringwork, adding tiny loops between curves. To finish, add tube 2 beading between petal curves at the cake base, and pipe tube 2 string bows around the cake top. Now position the lullabye cradle and insert flowers, having trimmed stems, along with ribbon and tulle. A sweet surprise for baby!

How to make baby's cradle

CUT CRADLE AND DRY. First roll out your mint sugar to ⅛-inch thickness; then place each cradle pattern piece over sugar and cut around it with a razor. Trim off any uneven edges with your razor and let cradle base and side pieces dry.

ASSEMBLE TWO SIDES FIRST. When all cradle pieces have dried, use Royal icing to glue the two straight side pieces to the base. Now prop sides up with cotton balls as shown and let dry in place. Now for the final step in assembling the cradle.

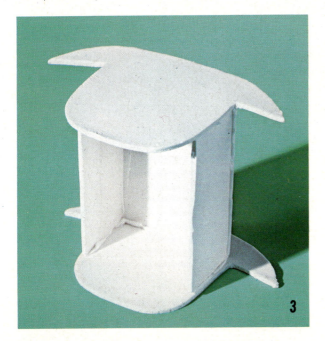

ATTACH ROCKER ENDS. Again using Royal icing, attach the two rocker ends of the cradle one at a time. When one is in place, turn the cradle upright so it rests on that end piece, then glue remaining rocker end. Let dry in this position as shown.

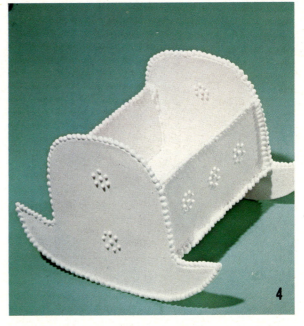

ADD DAINTY DECORATIONS. When dry, turn the cradle right side up and use tubes 1 or 2 and Royal icing to pipe the tiny beadwork trim. When you've added all the icing accents, cut a piece of styrofoam and place in cradle for adding flowers.

a showery parasol

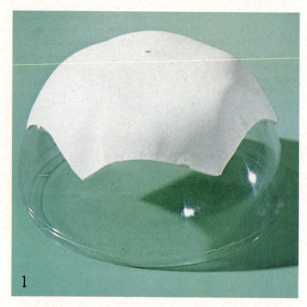

CUT AND DRY. Roll out mint sugar to ⅛-inch thickness and place parasol pattern on top. Cut around pattern with a razor; then while parasol is still moist, make a center hole and dry over a bowl or plastic ball mold that has a diameter of 4 to 5 inches.

ADD INSIDE TRIM. When parasol has dried, carefully peel it off the round form and turn it upside down. Now use Royal icing and tubes 1 or 2 to pipe pretty swirls of freehand icing designs as shown. After you've completed these decorations, you're ready for the next step.

ATTACH PARASOL HANDLE. Using Royal icing once again as an adhesive, attach a wooden stick or dowel rod to the center of the parasol. The handle for this parasol is 4¼ inches, but you may use any length you like. Let handle dry in place, then you're ready to finish.

TRIM PARASOL TOP. When the icing has dried and the handle is securely in place, turn the parasol right side up and stand in styrofoam. Then, with Royal icing, attach lace around the parasol edges and add tube 2 beading and gum paste forget-me-nots as shown.

How to decorate the cake

First make two mint sugar parasols and about one dozen gum paste daisies.

Bake a two-layer, 10-inch round cake and ice a bright green. Position it on an attractive serving plate and add the Royal icing trims. With a toothpick, mark the sides of the cake into twelve even-spaced divisions, then pipe a ribbed stripe with tube 2B at each marked point. Pipe puffy garlands with tube 20 between the stripes around both the top and bottom cake edges. Frame top garlands with tube 74, then edge base garlands with tube 74 at the top and tube 16 zigzag at the bottom. To finish, add a rosette with tube 20 at the top and bottom of each icing stripe; then position the parasols and flowers.

59

dainty heart boxes

Fanciful mint sugar heart boxes make table favors party guests are sure to fall in love with. Decorated with gum paste flowers, icing and ribbon they're ideal for holding candy, gifts and other treasures.

Just follow the step-by-step directions and soon you'll be making loving hearts like these for special friends and special times.

How to make small heart boxes

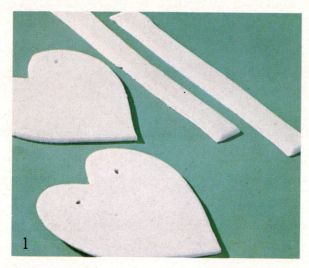

CUT AND DRY. Roll out mint sugar to ⅛-inch thickness and, using the heart patterns, cut out top, base and side pieces. With your small modeling stick, make two holes in both heart box top and base; then shape side piece around edges of base to form heart. Set all three pieces aside to dry.

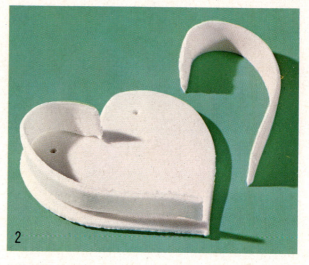

ATTACH SIDES. Edge the heart box base with Royal icing, then carefully attach the side piece as shown. Now let these two pieces dry and you're ready to add decorations and tie the heart box top in place.

TRIM HEART. Use tube 13 and Royal icing to make the pretty shell borders on the heart's sides and top. When you've piped the icing trimmings, make several gum paste rosebuds as shown on page 21. These will be used as additional decorations.

ADD RIBBON. After you've finished the icing decorations, thread a thin piece of satin ribbon through the holes in the heart box base. Thread this same ribbon through the heart top and tie in a bow to fasten in place. Now you can add buds and bows as shown on page 61.

How to make a large heart box

CUT AND ASSEMBLE. The large heart is made the same as the small boxes, except that you will use the large heart pattern. Roll out mint sugar to ⅛-inch thickness and cut out top, base and side pieces; then make two holes in both heart top and base and set aside to dry.

Assemble the large heart base and sides with Royal icing just as you did for the small heart shown on the opposite page. To decorate, pipe shell borders with tube 13, stringwork with tubes 1 or 2, then thread ribbon through heart top and base to fasten in place.

ADDING GUM PASTE TRIMS. To decorate the large and small heart tops, you will need to make about a dozen rosebuds and a half-dozen roses.

These flowers are made in a different way than regular roses. Form the center of the flower as directed in step three, page 13. Then add petals, cut with the rosebud cutter, just as you would for a regular rose.

You will also need to make several gum paste leaves using a small leaf pattern. When gum paste trims are dry, cut stems of flowers and leaves and position with Royal icing as shown. Add fluffy ribbon bows. To finish, pipe names on small hearts with tubes 1 or 2.

Fill the large box with pastel bon bons and chocolates as a gift to the guest of honor. The small heart boxes can serve as favors or place cards and hold nuts, mints or a little gift.

how to receive your diploma

Every student who has carefully studied the eight lessons in this book is eligible to receive a diploma upon providing proof of having acquired skill and proficiency in making gum paste flowers and trims. This you will be able to display with pride.

Here is what you need to do to receive your diploma:

1. Make one or more of each gum paste flower described in this book. All stems should be taped. The flowers are:

Calla lily	Rosebud
Spring blossom	Rose (any size)
Sweetheart rose	Petunia
Aster	Carnation
Daisy (any size)	Stephanotis
Chrysanthemum	Forget-me-not
Orchid (any size)	

2. Decorate at least one cake and trim it with gum paste flowers of your choice. The cake can be any size.

3. Make at least two of the mint sugar favors described in Lesson Eight. Trim with icing and gum paste flowers according to your own ideas—not necessarily in the way pictured in this book.

4. Take clear pictures of all the above (flowers, cake, favors) preferably in color. Please use a plain background, so that all the details of your work are clearly visible.

5. Send the pictures to:
   Wilton Enterprises, Inc.
   833 West 115th Street
   Chicago, Illinois 60643
   Attention: Gum Paste Diploma

(Please *be sure* to mark your envelope this way and *please print* your name the way you wish to have it appear on your diploma)

Your pictures will be carefully examined by a group of Wilton decorators. If the pictures show that you have achieved proficiency working with gum paste, your diploma will be mailed to you. It will be handsomely designed and signed by Josefa Barloco and Norman Wilton. Your diploma will be suitable for framing.

We look forward to awarding you a diploma, and are confident that you will not only achieve skill in the art of gum paste decoration, but will also have many years of pleasure and satisfaction in its practice.

Wilton Icing Recipes

BUTTERCREAM. Rich and creamy, this is the ideal icing for filling and frosting cakes and is fine for borders and stringwork too. Note: be sure to soften icing for chiffon and angel cakes. Recipe makes one cup and can easily be doubled.

⅓ cup butter or margarine, cold and firm
2 cups sifted confectioners sugar
½ teaspoon vanilla
1 or 2 tablespoons milk or cream

Place butter in a small bowl, and, using an electric mixer, beat several minutes until creamy. Add sugar, about ½ cup at a time and beat well after each addition. Add vanilla, then milk or cream, a little at a time and beat well. Store in an air-tight container in refrigerator and whip up before using again. For snow-white icing, use white vegetable shortening and butter flavoring.

ROYAL ICING. Smooth and hard-drying, this icing is perfect for decorating mint sugar favors or "show" cakes. Note: any grease will break this type of icing down, so keep utensils clean.

Royal Icing, Meringue

3 level tablespoons meringue powder
1 lb. confectioners sugar
3½ oz. warm water (slightly less than ½ cup)
½ teaspoon cream of tartar

Combine ingredients (mixing slowly), then beat at high speed for 7 to 10 minutes. (This recipe works best with a heavy-duty mixer.) Keep covered at all times with damp cloth. To restore texture later, simply rebeat. For lighter icing, add one tablespoon water, continue rebeating. Recipe yields 6 cups.

Royal Icing, Egg White

3 egg whites (room temperature)
1 lb. confectioners' sugar
½ teaspoon cream of tartar

Combine ingredients, beat at high speed for 7 to 10 minutes. Very quick-drying, so keep covered with damp cloth. Yields less volume than Royal icing made with meringue powder. Beating will not restore. Regular home mixer is adequate for this mixture. Exceptionally good consistency for borders and icing flowers. Yields 4 cups.

BOILED ICING. Satiny and smooth, this icing is also good for frosting and filling cakes, although it's not as rich-tasting as Buttercream. The Egg White version has a slightly better flavor—both versions make good borders and trims. Note; any grease will break this icing down, so keep utensils clean and greasefree.

Boiled Icing, Meringue

4 level tablespoons meringue powder
1 cup warm water
2 cups granulated sugar
¼ teaspoon cream of tartar
3½ cups sifted confectioners sugar

Boil granulated sugar, ½ cup water, cream of tartar to 240°. Brush sides of pan with warm water to prevent crystals. Meanwhile mix meringue powder with ½ cup water, beat 7 minutes at high speed. Turn to low speed, add confectioners sugar, beat 4 minutes at high speed. Slowly add boiled sugar mixture, beat 5 minutes at high speed. Keeps a week in refrigerator, covered with damp cloth. Rebeat before using again. Makes 4 cups.

Boiled Icing, Egg White

2 cups granulated sugar
½ cup water
¼ teaspoon cream of tartar
4 egg whites (room temperature)
1½ cups confectioners sugar, sifted

Boil granulated sugar, water, cream of tartar to 240°. Brush sides of pan with warm water to prevent crystals. Meanwhile whip egg whites 7 minutes at high speed. Add boiled sugar mixture slowly, beat 3 minutes at high speed. Turn to second speed, gradually add confectioners sugar beat all 5 minutes more at high speed. Cover with damp cloth while using. Re-beating will not restore texture. Makes 4 cups.

Josefa Barloco's bride's delight

Now that you know how to make Mrs. Barloco's favorite gum paste flowers and mint sugar decorations, she would like to share one of her favorite cake recipes with you. The cake is as delightful as it sounds and would make a perfect companion for a gum paste bouquet of flowers or a mint sugar parasol to present to a bride-to-be.

BRIDE'S DELIGHT CAKE
   4½ cups cake flour
   2½ cups sugar
   ½ teaspoon salt
   5 teaspoons baking powder
   ½ cup butter
   ½ cup shortening
   ¾ cup eggs
   ½ cup egg whites
   1¾ cup milk
   2 teaspoons vanilla

Sift flour, sugar, salt and baking powder twice. Place dry ingredients in bowl, add butter and shortening along with one cup milk. Beat until fluffy.

Add vanilla to the rest of the milk; then add eggs, milk and egg whites to the batter a small amount at a time. Beat until fluffy after each addition. After mixing all ingredients, beat at high speed until light and fluffy. Bake at 350 degrees for about 30 minutes until done. This recipe makes a 12" x 12" square cake or a two-layer 9" round cake.

PINEAPPLE FILLING
   ¾ cup granulated sugar
   3 tablespoons cornstarch
   2 tablespoons flour
   1¾ cup liquid
   2 egg yolks
   1 pound can crushed pineapple, drained

Add water to the juice of a one pound can of crushed pineapple to make 1¾ cup liquid. Add this liquid to the dry ingredients and cook until it thickens. Add egg yolks and cook another two minutes. Now add crushed pineapple and refrigerate overnight. Just before using, add juice of one lemon and some crushed cherries.

WHITE CLOUD FROSTING
   2½ cups granulated sugar
   ¾ teaspoon salt
   ¾ teaspoon cream of tartar
   ½ cup egg whites
   1 teaspoon vanilla
   1 heaping tablespoon glucose
   1 cup boiling water

Place all ingredients, except water in a double boiler. Mix thoroughly, add boiling water and immediately put over double boiler. Cook and beat mixture until it becomes very fluffy and forms peaks. Swirl on cake, using a soup spoon to form decorative puffs.